Foreword

Tourettes Action Chair of Trustees, Robin Paxton.

ME AND MY TOURETTE'S is a lovely and important book
that comes from both the head and the heart. Alfie's story is the story of many
thousands of children (and adults) who live with this difficult condition.
By explaining Tourette Syndrome, and showing how it feels to live with it,
Alfie shows us that having TS is just another way of being different.
ME AND MY TOURETTE'S doesn't make light of the condition.
It can be REALLY hard to cope with.
It gives us the facts. It shows us that the hardest part of living with
TS can be the reactions of others.
And its last words are perhaps the most important:

"Always remember to be kind."

To all children with Tourette Syndrome.

Written by Siânna Stodd

Illustrated by Gemma Denham

Published by Elizabeth Publications
Available from Amazon.com and other retail outlets
Available on Kindle and other devices

Hello, I'm Alfie. I'm eight years old
and I live with my Dad, Mum and little sister.

Look carefully, do you notice anything different about me?

Is it my hair? Or my eyes?
The colour of my skin?
How tall I am? What I'm wearing?

Do you give up?

Okay so maybe I've tricked you a little bit
because we are all very different on the outside,
as well as on the inside!

Everybody's brains are unique and work in different ways.
That is why you can't see what is special about me
straight away.

I have Tourette Syndrome.

Have you ever heard of it?
Do you know anyone else with it?

That's why it makes me feel quite special.
Only around one child in every hundred have it
and it's mostly boys!

So you're probably wondering what Tourette Syndrome is and how I got it?

Tourette Syndrome is a condition that is caused by the way my brain is organised.

Most people with Tourette Syndrome have tics. Tics are when your body makes movements and sounds that can't be controlled.

You can have tics at any age. One of my first tics that I remember doing was when I was about six and I would wave my hand in front of my eyes. I didn't even know that it was a tic at the time and I don't think anyone else noticed.

When I was seven, my dad, mum and teacher said
they'd seen me making different movements with my body.
I noticed this too but I didn't know why or how it was
happening and I couldn't stop it.

My parents took me to the doctor and he asked me what
movements I was doing and how often I was doing them.
He was very friendly and I found out that these movements
were my tics.

Want to know more?

People with Tourette Syndrome can't control their muscle movements or noises and are not doing them on purpose.

My tics often change and can be very fast, they can happen *again* and *again* and *again!*

Some of my tics are BLINKING, *sn-sn-sn*-sniffing, shoulder shrugging, tongue **CLICK CLICK CLICK**ing, throat clearing **AHEM AHEM,** jumping, **jerking,** *whistling,* animal sounds, eye rolling, **SHOUTING,** and saying the same word over and over over and over over and over over AND OVER AND OVER AND OVER AND OVER **AND OVER AGAIN!**

Maybe you could try to imagine how tiring this becomes for me every day and sometimes my tics can be painful.

I hope you're still paying attention;
you'll want to listen to this next bit...

The swearing tic.

This is just another type of tic and even though it's quite rare, it's the one everyone seems to know more about. Only around 10% of children with Tourette Syndrome have this tic.

The name for this type of tic is "coprolalia"
(cop – row – LA – lee – ya)

This is the tic I find most difficult. I will sometimes say rude and inappropriate words and it becomes extremely exhausting if I try to hold them in. I can't help it and I don't mean what I say. I always used to worry that I'd get into trouble at school, however my family, friends and teachers are really understanding and supportive about my Tourette's.

Want to know what it feels like?

I can stop my tics for a short time if I concentrate really hard, but this can feel very uncomfortable.

Try not to blink for a whole minute and you'll see how uncomfortable this feels.

Ready... Go!

Can you feel the pressure building up?
This feeling is used to describe how it feels to hold a tic in.
Imagine doing that over and over again every day!

What makes my tics worse?

If I'm worried or stressed, tired, hungry, excited
or if there are lots of changes going on!

What can make my tics better?

Being distracted or concentrating on a game or an activity.

I enjoy exercising, playing football or taking my dog for a walk. Having a good routine and getting a good night's sleep helps! Even though I like to stay up late at the weekends and play on my iPad!

I also have other symptoms alongside my tics that you can't always see. One of these is what I call my obsessions, where I experience lots of worrying thoughts, feelings and fears that something terrible might happen!

This can be very hard to explain to people as I find it tricky trying to understand it myself.

Do you think you have learned something
about me and my Tourette's?

I hope the answer is YES because it'd be great if you could
help someone else with Tourette Syndrome.

Here's some of the things you could do:

• Talk to them, be a good friend and help them to join in!

• Don't tell them to stop their tics

• Give them some time on their own if they
want to release some tics in private

• Try to be understanding and celebrate
each other's differences

• Raise awareness by telling your friends and
family about Tourette Syndrome

• And always remember to be kind!

Acknowledgements

A massive thank you to the beautifully talented Gemma Denham, who believed in the need for this book from the very beginning. I am grateful for your ability in bringing this book to life and creating characters in which children can find familiarity in.

A huge thank you to Rebecca Slorach for editing and supporting this book and ensuring every word is meaningful. Your exceptional advice, ideas and knowledge has been invaluable in piecing each page together.

And the greatest of thanks to George Szulczewski, for who this book was written for. You are adored by your family, friends and teachers and I am so privileged to have taught you. You continue to radiate positivity, show perseverance and humour, on your journey to understanding what makes you, you!

The world is a better place thanks to all the people who support, share and learn about Tourette Syndrome.

Made in United States
Troutdale, OR
12/16/2023

16055152R00021